DRAW & BE HAPPY

Art Exercises to Bring You Joy

Tim A Shaw & Cachetejack

ilex

An Hachette UK Company
www.hachette.co.uk

First published in Great Britain in 2018 by Ilex, an imprint of
Octopus Publishing Group Ltd
Carmelite House
50 Victoria Embankment
London EC4Y 0DZ
www.octopusbooks.co.uk

Publisher: Alison Starling
Editorial Director: Helen Rochester
Commissioning Editor: Zara Anvari
Managing Editor: Frank Gallaugher
Editor: Jenny Dye
Publishing Assistant: Stephanie Hetherington
Production Manager: Caroline Alberti

ISBN 978-1-78157-672-4

A CIP catalogue record for this book is available from the British Library.

Conceived, designed and produced by The Bright Press,
an imprint of The Quarto Group.

The Old Brewery, 6 Blundell Street,
London, N7 9BH, United Kingdom
T (0) 20 7700 6700 F (0) 20 7700 8066
www.QuartoKnows.com

The Bright Press
Ovest House, 58 West Street, Brighton,
BN1 2RA, United Kingdom

Publisher: Mark Searle
Associate Publisher: Emma Bastow
Managing Editor: Isheeta Mustafi
Senior Editor: Caroline Elliker
Art Director: Katherine Radcliffe
Layout and design: Plum Partnership Ltd.
Illustrations: Cachetejack

Printed and bound in China

10 9 8 7 6 5 4 3 2 1

CONTENTS

GET HAPPY   40

BUILD SELF-AWARENESS   62

ENERGISING   76

Get drawing if you want to get happy!

Perhaps you have picked up this book because you already know that when you are drawing, you feel happier, or when you have finished a piece of work, you get that glow of achievement. Or perhaps you aren't that into drawing yet, but the idea of sitting down to draw every day seems like something worth trying out.

The seventy-five exercises in this book are each completely different but they all have two things in common: they are designed to make you want to draw and to make you happy. If you need encouragement to flex your creative muscles, start with one of the warm ups that begin on page 10.

If you are feeling a bit down in the dumps and would like an instant pick-me-up, you will feel much better once you have taken time to find the joy in tiny things, as discussed on page 46.

Lots of people see being creative as a way to find a moment of calm in their lives. If that's you, turn to page 20, and start with some calming circles. If you have a nagging sense of longing for life to be different – better, bigger, braver or just. . .yes, different – then try some self-reflection. The exercises on pages 62–75 will help you figure out what's missing from your life right now.

There is no right or wrong way to use this book, to draw or to find happiness within yourself. So dig in anywhere. Find your best pencil, pen or paintbrush, and start drawing right now: on a scrap of paper, right across the walls of your room or out in the sunshine of a new day.

Go forth, draw and be happy!

A note from the author

I created the exercises in this book to inspire you to think about drawing as a daily tool – one that will encourage, comfort and stimulate you, and help you to plan and reflect.

Drawing can be about retaining control – the lines that you make on a surface will do as they are told and stay exactly where they have been placed – but drawing also has the potential to be fluid, free and liberating.

Your drawing surface can extend far beyond the boundaries of a sheet of paper, flowing out into the wider world. Anything you can imagine can become a drawing surface, and your drawing implement can be anything that will make a mark. There is no limit to potential subjects and you can be as inventive as you wish with your drawing process.

Drawing can be an independent or a collaborative activity, and it doesn't matter if you haven't sketched a thing since you were a child (although you may well already be scribbling, doodling and sketching without even realising it).

By challenging yourself with these exercises, I hope that you will find inspiration and creative happiness through drawing.

Tim A Shaw

UNTANGLE YOUR THOUGHTS

This is a very simple but satisfying way to warm up your drawing hand.

Sit somewhere comfortable with your pen and paper at the ready. Use the tip of your pen to follow an imaginary piece of string, and then make that line tie itself in a knot. Once you have made the knot, why not try getting more technical and letting your pen tie an overhand knot, a bowline, a half hitch, a sheepshank and a reef knot?

CONNECT WITH YOUR MATERIALS

**This is a quick exercise
to help you get a feel for the
surface you are drawing on.**

Applying firm pressure with a ballpoint pen, make a
mark from one side of your paper to the other (left
to right, or right to left). Working in one continuous
movement, make the line as straight as you can.

Then start again from the end point of your first line
and retrace your movement, trying not to deviate
from the original line at all. Now place your pen on
the original starting point once again and close your
eyes. Try to follow the line simply by feeling the slight
groove you have made in the paper. Focus on the
channel you previously forged with your pen and
let it guide your movement across the paper.

GET TO KNOW YOUR FRIENDS

**Start and finish a portrait
in the time it takes to count to ten.**

Take some time to study a friend's face. The aim is to capture every feature in the quickest, most efficient way possible. Without any breaks in your line, follow the shapes, shadows, lines and contours that make that person look different to any other. Try to limit yourself to ten seconds per portrait, concentrating on the person and not on the paper.

EVERYTHING IS CONNECTED

Without lifting your pen or pencil from the paper, mark out the outline of the room you are in. Don't only pay attention to the lines where the walls, floor and ceiling meet, but expand your awareness of your surroundings to record every piece of furniture, appliance, plug socket and light fitting.

Set yourself up to draw in an interior space. Look around you, paying particular attention to the multitude of interconnected lines that form the space. Use this exercise as a way of exploring the complex but functional maze of lines that make up the room you are in. Record on paper every change in angle and direction of the walls, the perspective of each light fitting and wall socket, the outline of each table or chair, and the dark shadows cast by objects and furniture. Once your drawing implement touches the surface of the paper, proceed without breaking the line. Let your hand follow the directions of the outlines within the room as you see them. Find the shortest, most efficient way of linking

lines that don't exist in the space – for example, from the corner of a wall to a light switch, or from the leg of a chair to the skirting boards. Each feature, fitting, wall and shadow should interlink to form one continuous, uninterrupted pencil trail.

If you prefer not to be sitting inside, use this same technique to capture the lines you see in a landscape, cityscape or the street you live on. Draw the silhouettes of buildings, the outlines of trees and the line of the horizon. Look for the interesting shapes and patterns made by road signs, road markings and trees. Just remember to keep your pen on the paper as you spot them.

A JOINED-UP WARM UP

A very simple and meditative warm up for your drawing hand.

Grab a pen with a fine nib and a large sheet of paper. Draw a line from left to right at the top of the paper. When you get to the end of the line, without breaking contact with the surface, double-back on yourself and continue the line as close to the first line as you can without touching. Continue down the paper. Each time you get near the edge of the paper, double-back in the opposite direction, never lifting the pen from the surface of the paper or touching the previously drawn line. Keep working to fill the page and create an intricate maze with your nib.

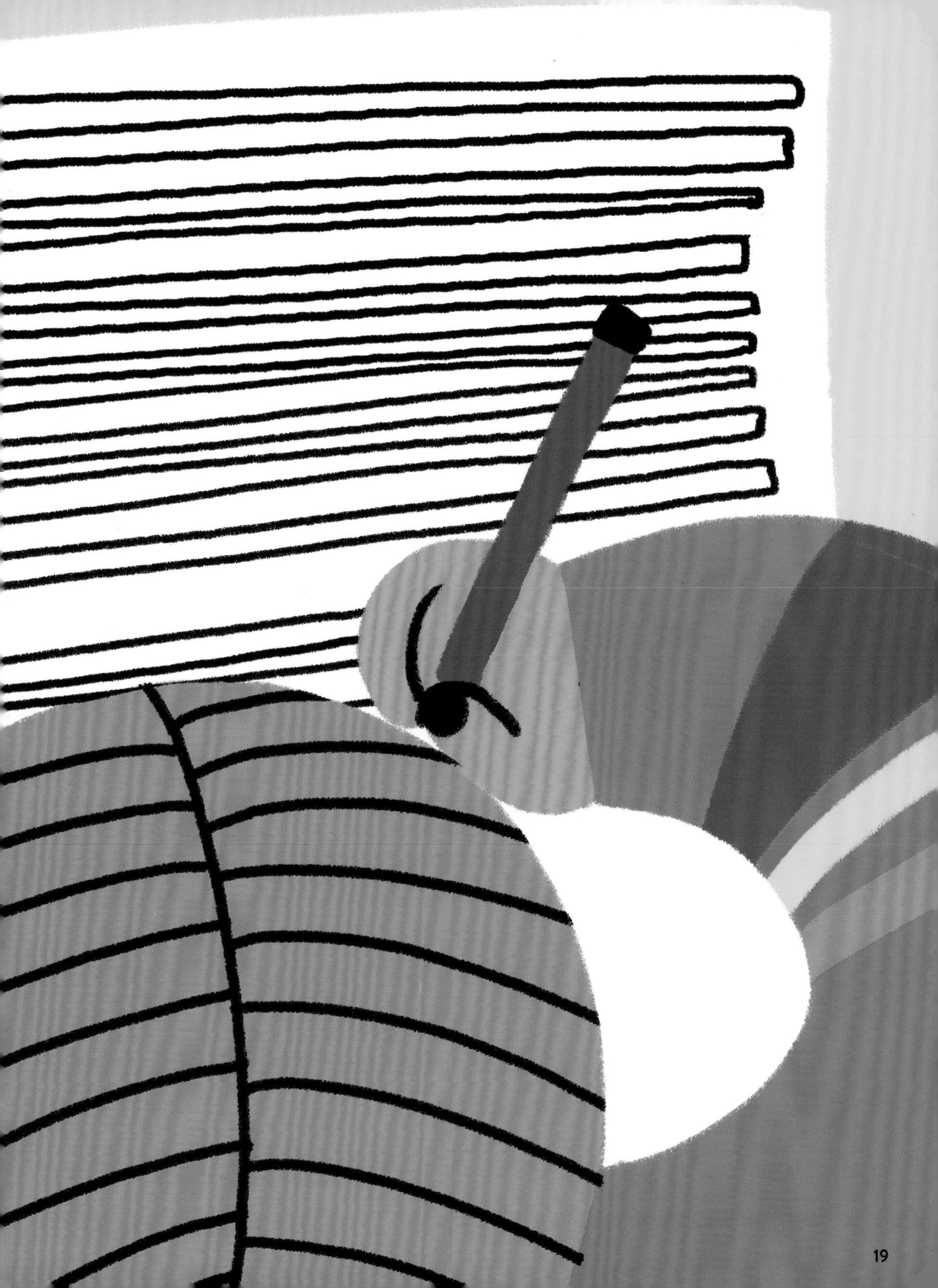

DRAW CIRCLES OF SERENITY

Silence your inner critic by developing the ability to let go of your impulse to overthink creativity, and learn to work intuitively instead.

Make circles on your paper, letting your hand move the pencil in smooth, confident motions to create the best circles that you can. Let the circles overlap, touch and stand alone. Speed up and slow down your motions. Make movements with your whole arm, then your hand, and then just your thumb and forefinger to mark out circles of different sizes. Allow yourself space and time to try this exercise, and repeat whenever you want a minute of calm.

Start here! Settle down to draw any object you have to hand. Before you put pen to paper, pause for a while to think about the colours of the subject you are going to draw.

Notice how each colour interacts with the space and other colours around it. Pay attention to how you respond to each colour.

When you are feeling overstimulated and unable to focus, try this meditative exercise.

MEDITATE ON COLOUR

You may realise that what you initially saw as a white, or red, or black object, is actually a collection of intricate colour networks that form fascinating compositions in themselves.

Remember that even the simplest subjects can be composed of an elaborate array of colours.

CALMING CURVES

**Let go of your worries by practising these simple
motions to create smooth, steady movements.**

Take your time and ease into this exercise. First,
draw a large circle that doesn't quite fill a sheet
of paper. Try to do this in one uninterrupted
movement, finishing the loop in the spot where
you started. If you use a square sheet of paper, this
will help to guide you, as the circle will come quite
close to the middle of the flat edge of the paper
on all four sides. Make sure you leave some space
around the circle, since you will need this later.

Soothing spirals
Next, make contact on the paper with your pen in
the middle of the circle you have just drawn, and
slowly open the shape outward as you spiral further
and further out from the centre towards the edges
of the large circle. The spiral can be as tight or as
open as feels natural to you, but make sure that as
it opens out fully it meets the curve of the inside of
the large circle perfectly. At this point, be careful
not to spin the paper, as there's a good chance you
might hypnotise yourself.

Lulling loops
Finally, start at a point on the outside of the circle
and make small, controlled loops that coil their
way around the entirety of the shape. Endeavour
to make each repetition as close to identical as
possible and again, try to make that last loop meet
perfectly with your first, as if it could continue
around indefinitely.

Try this any time you want a break—see how
perfect you can make these simple shapes.

Sometimes it can be difficult to get someone to sit still for a portrait. Many people feel self-conscious when they are being closely observed. Have a piece of paper and a short pencil in your jacket pocket, and the next time you are talking to someone when you are out and about, make a portrait inside your pocket. The difficult part is trying to observe your subject and translate features onto the paper while also enjoying and participating in a social interaction.

LISTEN, LOOK, DRAW

You will, hopefully, capture a genuine impression of the person in front of you, while engaging in conversation! This exercise works best if you have a small sketchbook or notepad with a hard back to it. There needs to be some structure to the surface you are drawing on, to avoid jabbing yourself with your drawing implement if the tip or nib breaks through the paper surface. Make sure the pencil or pen kept ready and waiting in your pocket is nice and short, too.

When you have chosen your subject, don't let them know that they are about to be a model for a miniature portrait. This way you will get their natural expression, without any self-conscious pouting or posing.

Follow the features of your unwitting model's face with your eyes and with your hand simultaneously. You may have to work quickly, as it can be difficult keeping up a conversation and making an accurate depiction of a face without looking at your work.

You may want to give your subject the portrait when you leave, although have a look at it first, just in case it isn't completely flattering.

FOCUS ON THE DETAIL

Use your pen or pencil to draw someone's hair. Relax and feel the movement in your whole body as your drawing hand mirrors the flow and change in direction of each strand. Continue doing this, capturing on paper every length of hair on their head, from root to tip. The subject doesn't have to be human, either. Your model could be a dog, a cat or a squirrel, if you can get them to stay still for long enough. . .

Choose a subject – with hair or fur – who is likely to sit still for a good period of time. This could be a partner who is watching a film or has fallen asleep on the couch, or a relaxed (or taxidermied) pet. Notice that what is perceived of as a lock of hair is actually hundreds or thousands of individual strands that interlock, weave and intertwine.

Start this seemingly impossible task by choosing a specific point at the follicle of one shaft of hair and follow the strand with your eyes and your drawing implement simultaneously. As each hair becomes lighter or darker along its length, mimic the changes in tone by applying more or less

pressure to your surface. Only put on paper what you can see, so if a hair disappears behind another, mark the surface in the same way. The resulting drawing should represent the shape and contours of your subject without the need for any other discernible features. See if you can describe a sense of movement and character to convey the subject's individuality.

Remember, you don't just have to choose the hair on someone's head. The same exercise can be effective when studying the hairs on an arm, hand or beard.

BE A FEARLESS EXPLORER

Even a white-painted wall can be a fascinating landscape to explore.
Focus in on something that you would normally consider dull or forgettable,
and reinterpret it on paper as if you are an explorer in uncharted territory. Record every
dimple or lump as if it were a valley or mountain in a newly discovered landscape.

Choose an ordinary object near you as your unexplored territory. Before you begin to draw, take some time to notice the small details in the materials that make up this object. When we see a white-painted wall in a bedroom, a wooden desk in an office, the floor tiles in a corridor, or the side of a cardboard box, we register these surfaces as flat and seemingly two-dimensional. We concentrate on the picture hanging on that wall, the lamp sitting on the desk, the pattern on the floor tiles and the writing on the side of the box.

Unseen topographies

If you look closely at these surfaces, you will see that they are, in fact, anything but flat. The thick-pile roller that applied the emulsion paint to the surface of the plaster will have left thousands of tiny mountains and valleys. Craters will have formed where minuscule air bubbles developed and popped in the paint before it dried, giving the wall a texture similar to the surface of the Moon.

Floor tiles, although they have a very tight weave, are a jungle of synthetic fibres that hook and intertwine to create the appearance of a smooth and solid surface. The wood grain on a desk can be a three-dimensional map of a hilly landscape, and a cardboard surface is actually covered in pores and spiky brown hairs.

Closely explore the terrain of a seemingly flat surface and create a drawing that exaggerates the peaks and troughs, the textures and terrains, and the tiny imperfections. Approach the task as if you are creating an artwork of a vast, sprawling landscape.

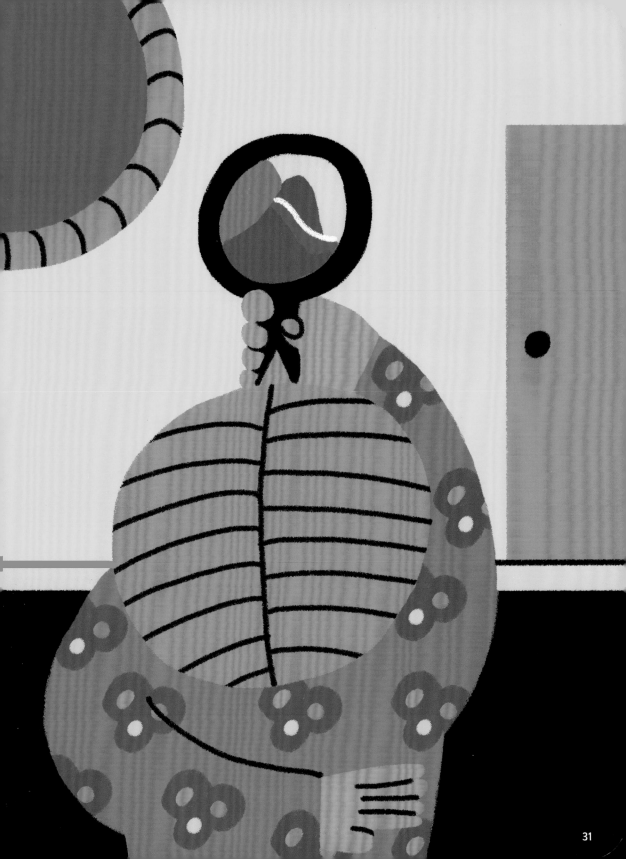

CURATE SERENDIPITY

Dedicate a sketchbook to the collection and cataloguing of tea and coffee stains. Whenever you see (or have left) a mark from a hot drink on a kitchen surface, on your desk or on a restaurant table, record the shape it leaves.

Starting with a small, preferably square, sketchbook, keep a journal that records all the cup stains that you encounter day to day. Instead of viewing them as an annoying mess that needs to be cleaned up immediately, turn your thinking around and embrace these accidents as sketching opportunities. Some marks will be neat, symmetrical circles, some will be faint crescents, and some will be solid and surrounded by drips, splatters and spills. Each residual shape tells a micro-story and is evidence of an action and even an individual's personality.

Using a pen, draw the outline of the mark left by the cup, then add each splash, drop or spill with a series of circles, tear shapes and amorphous blobs.

Try to work to scale and place every mark in exactly the same position as it appears on the stain.

If you want a speedier way of recording these unique shapes, you could make your own sketchbook diary by binding or stapling sheets of tracing paper together. You will then be able to open up the book and lay a page down on a surface to trace around the stains. Make sure the cup marks are dry, unless you don't mind a few wrinkly pages and a book with a faint scent of coffee.

DECONSTRUCT AN OBJECT

Think about how an object is made up. What makes it the shape that it is? What makes it work? Draw a still life composed of all the parts of an object. If you choose a TV, draw all the individual components that make it work, from the wiring to the screws to the LEDs. If you choose a bicycle, make a drawing that deconstructs and reconstructs every cog, chain and spoke.

Breaking down any task into smaller pieces is a good way to calm your worries. Here, you are breaking down your subject instead. Decide which object you are going to visually deconstruct and take a moment to identify all of its component parts and the shapes they form. For instance, if you were to break down a skateboard into all its individual components, it would illustrate how simple and effective the design really is. You would be left with a deck, the grip tape, two trucks, four wheels, and various pads, axles and hardware. On the other hand, if you were to break down a car, you may have thirty thousand individual parts, and you would need a lot of paper and several months of work to record and draw every piece.

Choose an object that fits with how adventurous you are feeling, how confident you are in your drawing skills and how much patience you have. Rather than creating a visual list of each individual part, approach your composition as if you were creating a still life of these individual elements. Imagine how you would light the scene, how one screw might cast a shadow on another, or how the spoke on a wheel may partially obscure a handle positioned behind it.

If you can, you may want to physically deconstruct your subject and then set up a scene from all of its parts so that you can represent it accurately on paper.

Concentrate all of your attention to detail to make a micro-drawing of a rolling landscape, creating the biggest scene on the smallest sheet of paper.

EVERYTHING YOU IN THE PALM OF

Using a pen with a fine point and a small piece of paper or card, draw the expansive landscape as minutely and intricately as you can. Don't let the size of the drawing hold you back – use the small size of the surface you are drawing on as a way of focusing on every detail you want to record. As you find focus, the rest of the world fades away. Think about who you want to see the finished result, and work to create an entire landscape for them to explore.

CAN SEE YOUR HAND

FROM DARK TO LIGHT

If you have ever witnessed a particularly dramatic thunderstorm, you may have noticed how, for the split second when lightning strikes, night can turn to day. Suddenly a landscape can be seen, just momentarily, in the middle of the night. This is the perfect sketchercise if you are struggling to sleep.

The pigment Vantablack absorbs more than 99.9 per cent of visible light. If you were to make a sculpture that was covered in it, you wouldn't be able to discern a single feature with the naked eye. It can be disconcerting to experience pitch blackness; it is an experience that most people do not have. Even when it seems as though it is as dark as it can get, when the lights are turned off at night, if there's a power cut in the building, or in a rural street with no street lamps or light pollution, as soon as our pupils dilate and our eyes adjust, we can start making out shapes.

For this exercise, you will need to adjust to the darkness, without squinting or straining your eyes, to be able to register the faint outlines and forms in front of you.

Put yourself in a situation where it seems to be completely dark. It may well be too dark to see your sketchpad and pencil. Create a drawing that represents the shapes that emerge from the darkness – you may have to do this by feeling your way around the paper. When you find somewhere with proper lighting, whether it is the brightness of the next day or when you move into another room, use your imagination to fill out the whole scene, picturing what you might have seen if there had been a lightning flash in the distance or if the lights had flickered on while you were drawing. Then go back and look at that view in the light of day, and see how closely your drawing relates to reality.

DREAM BIG

Focus your mind and energy by creating a detailed drawing of the biggest, grandest, most opulent home you can imagine. The only catch is: the entire drawing has to be no bigger than a postage stamp.

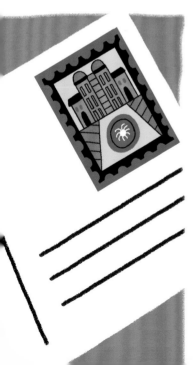

This is a chance to build your dream house without any restrictions on space and with no limit to what you put in it. In most towns and cities, house prices are rising and the amount of living space available per person is decreasing. If you live in a small flat, you have to be economic with your space and your possessions. In some ways that can be a good thing – if you are able to live without too much stuff it can have a positive effect on the environment and potentially on your mental health. It can also be a good incentive to get out more and see friends and family. However, most people at some point have dreamt of having their own palatial space to live in.

Rather than having a small refrigerator, you could have three walk-in freezers in a kitchen that is itself the size of a four-bedroom house. And why restrict yourself to just one kitchen when you could have eight – one for each day of the week and one extra just for making apple crumble? Of course, when you throw a party for all of your friends in the ballroom, they'll need a place to stay and will each need their own bedroom with en suite facilities. All of

those bedrooms and kitchens will make for one very large house.

Now that you have fired up your imagination, prepare your drawing surface by cutting out a small section of paper or marking out a small rectangle in portrait or landscape mode to form the parameters of your drawing. Use a fine-tipped pen or the sharpest pencil you can find to draw the biggest mansion, stately home or castle, complete with towers, turrets, an east wing, a west wing and a drawbridge. Include all of the windows (even if they will only be discernible as tiny pencil specks on the front of your building), a driveway that is big enough to accommodate your collection of cars, and the flag that, when flying at full mast, signals

that you are in residence. Depending on how good your eyesight is, you may need a magnifying glass to help you to draw, and certainly anyone looking at your drawing will need a magnifying glass to see it properly.

Maybe you are perfectly happy with your home as it is. In this case, see this as an exercise in controlling and perfecting your skills in drawing intricate details. However, if you dream of one day living in your own castle, you could treat your stamp-sized rendering of this imaginary Lilliputian manor as a plan to hand to an architect in the future. You never know, maybe one day you will build it to full size.

FOLLOW THE LIGHT

Everywhere you look there are incredible artworks being created by light reflecting, refracting and diffracting. Watch out for this enchanting light show.

To record the light show that's visible around you, first take a look and notice the way that light alters the objects that you see. There may be a band of white reflecting on the kitchen surface, or a shimmer refracted through a glass of water. Watch out for a flash of light captured on the corner of a bottle or the bonnet of a car, or a sparkle on a paper clip on your desk.

Draw a series of shapes, lines and gestures to represent the way that light reacts as its source moves, vibrates, retracts or is obstructed.

This exercise can work equally well by observing and capturing shadows formed by an object obscuring the light. As the source of light or even the object itself moves, follow the shadow's journey on your paper. Notice that the shadow isn't just one shade – it is made up of different levels of darkness, and you can replicate this by adjusting the amount of pressure you apply when adding shading to the shapes.

You can make life easier for yourself by choosing to set up your paper in a position that allows light and shadows to sit on its surface, and then trace the projected shapes with your pencil. Then, as the shapes move, retrace the outlines to form a moving artwork that documents the passage of light. Of course, if the light source is stationary (like a lamp), you can always cheat and move it yourself!

INCREDIBLE

Over time, it can be easy to overlook some of the extraordinary sights, people and moments that you encounter as you follow your daily routine. This exercise is a prompt to get excited about the place where you live by making a record in the form of a small drawing each time you notice something new.

To make a visual record of every incredible thing you see, as you see it, you will need to spend the next week acting like a tourist – or even an alien from another planet – visiting the place where you live. Look up, to the tops of buildings and the sky; look down, to the ground beneath your feet; sit in a park or coffee shop and watch your fellow citizens move through the space; notice any wildlife and how it interacts with its surroundings.

EVERY DAY

Keep a pen or pencil and a sheet of paper in your pocket, purse or rucksack at all times. It doesn't matter if the paper gets folded or creased, just make sure it is to hand when you need it.

No matter how fleeting the moment or small the sight, put it down on paper in the form of a drawing – work in a way that will allow a full seven days of drawing on a single sheet of paper. Treat the paper that you are carrying as if it were a photo album that you are filling with a series of incredible micro-moments recorded using a pen rather than a camera.

THE JOY OF TINY THINGS

**Focus on the tiny, intricate details
of something very close to you.**

Examine the small indentations on the surface of a desk,
the marks and scratches on a wall, or the angles and reflected
light on the nib of your pen.

Using a sharp pencil or a fine-tipped pen, capture all of these
minute, and normally overlooked, details in a precise drawing.

FIND BEAUTY IN A REFLECTION

Beautiful reflections can easily go unnoticed. It might be the sky and lampposts that have been warped and curved on the rear windscreen of a car, or the distorted bodies of pedestrians on the surface of a pond in the park. Capture these alternative views of the world in the form of drawings, translating the surreal shapes, double images and refracted light to paper.

Change the way in which you look at shiny surfaces and concentrate on the bowed, warped, elongated and shortened imagery that they create. You can find joy in the most mundane things if you view them this way. Our eyes can become tuned to focusing on the solid, choosing to recognise the important shapes and colours of, say, cars and houses, and the people within. Of course, this is essential and allows us to function safely and effectively. We look through windows, at the contents of a glass, and register the handle of a car door. But there is a beauty in the reflections on the windows, the play of light on a glass of water, and the distorted imagery captured on the spray-painted surface of the car door that we can overlook.

Choose a stationary subject with a smooth surface and look carefully at the contours and character of the reflected image. Translate the surreal shapes, double images and refracted light to create a drawing that captures an alternate view of the world. See if you can create an impression of the object only through the reflections on it. Hopefully the result will be a surrealist masterpiece, or at the very least, something that resembles a fun-house mirror.

KEEP A RECORD OF IMPORTANT THINGS

Give yourself some time to put down on paper all of the things that are most important to you. This visual list may be comprised of valuable belongings, precious possessions, your house and even your friends. Include the items, people and places to which you have an emotional attachment. As you draw all of these meaningful things, think about the detail of what makes each one so important to your happiness.

Before making a drawing that represents them, think about the most significant things in your life. If you were to wake up today and undertake the most thorough spring clean, going through everything that you own, rummaging through every single item and being ruthless about what to keep and what to throw away, what would you be left with?

A visual legacy

Imagine what a stranger would think if they were to look through all of your remaining possessions. They would probably question why you would want to hold on to a jumper with a hole in the collar, a collection of matchboxes and a box full of photographs that are stuck together. It is likely that for you, the value of these objects is much more than the sum of their parts. Each kept object serves as evidence of your past and is loaded with memories and meaning.

A personal treasure map

Rather than having each item floating in the white space of the paper, form links between the objects, and build a personal narrative around them. Perhaps you could order them in a timeline, taking into account when each was acquired – or maybe you want to position each on a map of the world. Remember, you don't only have to draw objects that you possess. There may be an incredible sculpture in a museum that you make a trip to visit once a year, or a hill or street that you used to run up or down at the age of five that formed an important part of your childhood.

SMALL AND WONDERFUL

Taking time to really focus in on a tiny object is a revealing and rewarding exercise. Choose something really, really small, whether it's an eyelash, a lemon pip or the tip of your shoelace. Imagine what it would look like under a microscope, and make an intricate drawing of the atoms, microbes or bacteria that make it look the way it does.

Is there something tiny that has always made you wonder what makes it the way it is? To replicate what you imagine a tiny subject would look like if you were to study it in depth and detail, you will need to consider the microscopic components that give it its colour, shape and texture.

If you take artist's paint as an example, the same beautiful pigments that give a paint its colour, when milled into different shapes, will emit different colours to the human eye. If you were to look at grains of sand under a microscope, they might well look like a visual cacophony of vibrant shells, hard sweets, shards of glass and minuscule glossy planets.

Draw the equivalent of a microscope slide's worth of your subject's detail on your sheet of paper. Imagine the shapes of the elements, and think about whether they might correspond to the shape of the object as a whole. What will the colours be, and will you express them by adding colour to the drawing or by changing the depth or shading? Will all the tiny pieces that make up the object be more visually stunning than what you can see on its surface?

DESIGN HAPPINESS

Design a tool that will bring you happiness. It could be a single implement or it could be based on a Swiss army knife, with many different facets, each one included to help you to have a better day.

For your prototype drawing of a device that allows all your small pleasures to be readily to hand, think about all the rituals and activities you undertake to create happy moments in your daily life. Perhaps you play music when you get out of bed, take photographs of small dogs when walking to work, go for runs in the rain or order boxes of sweet and salty popcorn when you go to the cinema. All of these small pleasures may be tools to make sure that your week is going to be a good one.

Work it out
Start with something that looks like the body of a Swiss army knife, replacing the blades, screwdrivers, scissors and corkscrew with speakers for your music, a camera, a box of popcorn, a musical instrument and a pair of trainers. There might be secret compartments that can hold slices of toast, and even a pocket that contains your sketchbooks and pencils. Your tool design will be unique to you and will almost certainly include implements that no one else would think of.

If you were to build this happiness tool to scale, it could be as big as a garden shed, so it might be best to keep it as a work on paper, for now. . .

INNER HAPPINESS

Picture the innermost thing you can think of. Is it something secret and hidden, something that exists in a physical form or something spiritual? Perhaps it's the core of the Earth, thousands of kilometres below where you stand.

Depicting your choice of the innermost thing on paper can be challenging: what image comes into your mind? Does it clearly and physically manifest itself, or is it more of a sensation that is difficult to describe in words or pictures?

Is it something vast in area like the core of the Earth, trapped beneath the boiling and bubbling outer core and layers of mantle and crust? Perhaps it is microscopic in size, smaller than an atom and at the very centrepoint of the Universe. Or maybe what you are picturing is harder to visualise. It could be a feeling in your stomach, an emotion that can't be described or even a thought or an idea that is being worked through in the back of your brain.

Translating thoughts to paper

The challenge is to represent these thoughts using a pen and paper. How can you make visual something that might be conceptual? Try to assign a colour to the innermost thing, imagine how the texture might feel, and think about what the concept or item represents and how you could depict this in two dimensions.

Whether your drawing results in a speck, an elaborate network of cells or a portrayal of a thought process, look back at what you have drawn and reflect on how you have managed to convey something so big or so small with just a few marks on paper.

AS FAR AS YOU CAN REACH

Now that you have made a drawing of the innermost thing that you can think of, try the same exercise with the outermost thing. Depending on your viewpoint and mood, your drawing may be of the furthest galaxy in the Universe or of the garden fence. Is your outermost vision epic and infinitesimal or ordinary and everyday?

What place, entity or sensation is furthest from you? Perhaps the outermost thing that you can think of at this moment is actually quite close to you: the top layer of clothing that you are wearing or the boundary of a sports field. It might be a feeling of freedom or the limits of the sky. Or you might be thinking of the edge of a galaxy billions and billions of light years away.

Use light and shadow to depict space, or convey a feeling through abstract shapes and forms. Alternatively, you may be able to portray your thoughts effectively with a representative drawing of an object or place.

Whatever the resulting picture depicts, compare your drawing of the outermost thing with your previous drawing of the innermost thing. Are there similarities between the two? Do both represent space and the unknown or something much smaller? Or have you approached this exercise in a completely different way, with a completely new result?

THE ENCHANTMENT OF SOMETHING CLOSE

There are countless incredibly beautiful things that can be represented on paper. And it may be that there is something worth recording right in front of you. Portray an object that is in your current field of view, especially if that something would not normally seem an obvious choice for the subject of an artwork.

To capture an immediate object in your drawing, you will need to visually describe the way that the light reflects off its surface – if at all, study any complex shapes and shadows, and explore the textures and intricacies that transform the object into a fascinating artefact worth preserving on paper.

Ordinary beauty

Walk through a large art museum and you are sure to see galleries filled with hundreds of incredible paintings, drawings and sculptures depicting breathtaking vistas, impressive architecture, fascinating characters and thoroughbred horses. There may well also be a number of artworks that represent less obvious subjects, though still rendered on paper or canvas with no less thought or love. Shiny apples, bunches of grapes, humble spoons, chicken bones, wicker baskets and even chamber pots have all been immortalised in paint or charcoal and then displayed, studied and enjoyed by generations of art lovers.

Look to your immediate vicinity and study any objects within it. If you are sitting at a desk, there may be a loose staple, a pen lid or an offcut of tape, all within reach. If you are sitting on a park bench, items with fascinating stories may surround you: how did that single left-hand glove get left behind? Who stuffed their banana peel in a coffee cup and balanced it on the back of the bench? How long has it taken the chocolate bar wrapper lying by your feet to fade to almost white? All these stories are worth telling.

GET REACQUAINTED

A self-portrait can reveal a lot about your inner life and the persona you present to the world. Concentrating on the internal rather than the external can produce valuable insight.

The object of this exercise is to use drawing to find a unique, personal way to reveal something about yourself. Approach constructing a self-portrait as an exercise in communicating something that is particular to you.

There is a skill in being able to capture a realistic likeness of a subject – the correct positioning of facial features, the contours on the surface of the skin, the bone structure and shadows under the eyes, and the movement of thousands of strands of hair. However, there is another skill in capturing something beyond what can be seen on the surface of a person's body. When you look at a portrait, you want to discover something about the subject: something complicated, passionate, troubled or joyful conveyed through an expression or hidden in their eyes. A lifetime of experiences and emotions can be captured in a portrait to create a fascinating visual biography. Before starting to draw yourself, think about what you want to convey and how you want to go about doing it. Maybe it is easiest to start by looking in a mirror, or at the back of your hand, or at the clothes you are wearing. Spend some time closely scrutinizing each mark, scar, line or tattoo on your skin. Consider the choices you have made in what you are wearing. Or you might want to start drawing and see what happens.

A unique perspective

Concentrate on certain facial features or the way you choose to present yourself through your clothes, but as you continue to draw, try to represent something unique about yourself. Perhaps something you hadn't noticed or realised about yourself before. This can be something subtle – for instance, a slight asymmetry to your smile or a cluster of new laughter lines, which can be conveyed through applying soft markings to the paper or the use of subtle gradations of colour. If you are portraying your character as being full of energy, frustration or excitement, this can be achieved with big, rough gestural marks and the use of strong darks and lights or with vibrant, contrasting colours. Think about what to place in the background of your drawing – you can use a landscape or you can surround yourself with objects that symbolise something under the surface that you want to express.

Consider the viewer

Also, consider the way your represented self interacts with the viewer – do your eyes meet the gaze of a viewer, or do they stare into the distance? The colours you choose will carry messages about how you want to be seen – warm and inviting or harsh and jarring. Give yourself enough space and time to work on your portrait, and use this exercise as an opportunity not to be self-conscious, but to be conscious of yourself.

You don't have to get the anatomy of your face exactly right – your self-portrait can be abstract, expressiv, or made up of simple shapes and a creative use of colours. You might feel that you can make a portrait out of many different elements, or you might want to use symbols to express something that makes you who you are. Most importantly, remember that if you were to repeat this exercise tomorrow, the results would be entirely different.

A PERSONAL LIGHT SHOW

The visual patterns that seem to move across the backs of our eyelids when we close our eyes are called phosphenes. Transferring these abstract patterns to paper will encourage you to concentrate on a vision that is not produced by light.

Close or cover your eyes and focus on the shapes that appear as if projected onto the insides of your eyelids. Sometimes the shapes are easy to make out; at other times, they may seem unintelligible. What you are seeing may look like a charge of light or electricity beating or pulsating on the other side of your eyelid, or it could seem as though there is a network of veins or a galaxy of stars panning across your vision.

After spending some time concentrating on all that is happening when your eyes are closed, memorise these shapes and moving sensations and represent them in a drawing on your paper. When you have your eyes closed, try to think of the light coming from inside your eyes, rather than from the space around your physical self. These electrical charges that are being produced by you are creating beautiful, abstract, kaleidoscopic matrices and, although it is impossible to fully recreate the sensation, there is an opportunity to make a complex and beautiful artwork from these perceptions. Think of the border shape of the impression you are making, too – it might not be the same shape as the paper. Carefully consider how you will convey movement and use your pen to direct the flow of shapes and colours across the surface.

THE STORY IN YOUR HANDS

The cracks, scars, crevices and blemishes on our hands tell a distinctive personal narrative. Write your own story by examining the back of your hand, then transferring each and every discernible feature to paper.

Before you embark on an obervational, exploratory drawing of your hands, take a look at your non-dominant hand. Do the marks, lines and scars prompt memories?

Spend some time getting reacquainted with this part of your body. Are your nails perfectly rounded, buffed and manicured, or are they chipped or showing the telltale signs of a nail-biting habit? Do the wrinkles on your knuckles form loose circles, or do they look more like a network of veins on a dried-out leaf? Maybe the shape of your dorsum (the back of your hand) is long and contoured, or perhaps is it robustly square. Does your hand show signs of wear from hard physical work, or is it soft and unblemished?

Build a narrative

Rather than following the standard rules for mapping out the shape of a hand and planning out a series of lightly sketched squares, circles and curves, start at the beginning of your hand story – the tip of your little finger. Follow the crescent shapes of your nails down past your cuticles and continue to study each line, shadow and mark as you explore your way around your hand. Transfer all of these unique features to paper by applying a series of scratches, flicks and brush movements with your pencil. Rather than filling in the gaps in your drawing with pencil marks, shading and cross-hatching, draw only what you have observed, accentuating any features and traits that recount incidents or journeys your hand has been through.

Hands of time

It doesn't matter if the hand you draw isn't to scale or anatomically accurate, as long as you capture the unique traits that make your hand remarkable. When you have finished the drawing, there should be no doubt that the subject belongs to you, and it might be able to help you recollect moments from your past. Imagine what the drawing would look like if you made it twenty years from now and how much your hands will go through before that time.

You might not have ever looked this closely at your hands. They are probably too busy doing things. Because of this they are often full of character and may hold evidence of acts that you have long forgotten.

CELEBRATE HOW YOU SEE IT

The next time you travel away from home, rather than sending a postcard that you buy, make your own. Document your experience of a place or event to create a unique record of your trip.

Forget the idealised tourist views and standard sand-and-sea postcard compositions: instead, concentrate on portraying your own perspective and experience of the place you are visiting – whether positive, negative or ambiguous, telling your personalised holiday story to family and friends.

Whether you are sunning yourself on a beach holiday, away on a work trip in a new city or visiting family in a nearby town, you may be in the habit of sending a postcard back home to let someone know you are thinking of them. The postcards available for sale on the rotating stands in the average tourist shop usually depict an idealised seascape, landscape or cityscape, with accentuated colours and perspective. At the same time, they can often also look a bit tired, faded or out of date, and are often rather ugly.

Most art materials shops stock a wide range of sketchpads, and many will carry postcard-size pads of watercolour paper, often with the address lines and stamp outline printed on the reverse of each sheet. Take one of these postcard pads with you the next time you are out of town and make your own postcard that describes the place you are visiting.

A unique perspective

Draw a seagull stealing your sandwich, a busker playing a saxophone, the view from your hotel window or the condensation on the side of a cold drink. Then address it, stamp it and send it on its way.

If you don't have the correctly sized pad, buy a standard tourist postcard and, rather than writing a short message to the recipient in the left-hand side of the reverse of the card, make a little sketch that visually describes what you would have written instead.

ANIMATE YOUR LIFE

Make a flip book that begins with a sketch of yourself as a baby and continues to illustrate your growth through childhood, adolescence, adulthood and on to old age. Use this exercise to reflect on how much you have changed and all of the new experiences that are yet to come.

For your lifetime's flip book, you will need a soft-backed sketchbook with thin or lightweight paper stock, or you could make your own book by stapling approximately thirty sheets of paper together along one edge. The booklet will need to be easy to flip through and small enough to ensure the pages have enough structure so as not to fold and flap when being flipped.

Begin at the end

Begin on the final page by drawing yourself as an old person, perhaps holding a walking stick and slightly bent forward. Use simple lines to convey your grand age and wisdom. Turn to the next page and through the thin paper you should be able to see the faint outlines from your first drawing. Draw a similar image that is very slightly more upright with a touch more hair or with one less wrinkle. Continue the backward progression

through the pages, always using the previous page as a guide. Imagine you are regaining three years per page, so over the thirty pages of the book you will be spanning ninety years of life.

Fly through time

Four pages in, you may lose the walking stick, and six pages further, your drawn self may be a little taller with fewer facial lines. On the final pages, as you move back through adolescence and childhood, your drawings will gradually diminish in size until, by the final page, you are a tiny newborn baby. If you used each previous drawing as a guide, as you flick through the book there should be a smooth, animated snapshot of your life.

You can flip either way, so you can see yourself getting younger or older, as the mood takes you.

ONE HUNDRED LEGS

It can be fun to visualise living in the world as a completely different being. Imagine yourself as a one-hundred-legged creature with your head and upper body unchanged. Create a drawing that shows how fifty pairs of limbs might propel you through life.

Start by drawing yourself from the waist up, and then add leg after leg after leg. How you fit them on the page is up to you, whether you snake around the sheet, spiral towards the centre of the paper or continue to a second page. Maybe all the legs are in a huge bundle, or maybe they form a circle around your head.

FANTASTIC DRAWINGS

Find a way of transcribing something from your imagination or a dream onto paper. Use this exercise as an opportunity to think up a new way of making marks on paper. Transfer the feeling of ethereal, surreal or fantastical thoughts through drawing.

Think about how you might be able to portray a dream that is not intrinsically visual. Some people wake up and can clearly remember their dreams. To those people, dreaming can seem as real as waking life. Others may remember certain partially formed scenes from their dreams, with people and elements clearly situated within an expanse of vague, unformed space. Then there are people who, when they wake up, may not remember anything that can be easily described but are instead left with a feeling – an impression or a sense that something has happened, but that remains undefined and out of reach. Even a memory without a visual element can have a powerful impact on the beginning of the day.

More than what you see

How can you convey a sensation by using only a pencil and paper? Will the resulting drawing be purely abstract, or will you find a way of using imagery from real life to communicate an atmosphere or emotion? What marks and gestures could you use to most effectively represent a state of mind?

Perhaps you will be able to find a way of communicating what is in your head more effectively with drawing than you would by using words.

ENJOY THE JOURNEY

The next time you are a passenger on a long journey, keep yourself energised by using your time to document all that is going on outside the window.

Keep a separate sketchbook to take with you on all your journeys, whether you travel by car, train, plane or bus. That way, rather than falling asleep or staring blankly at the road markings zooming by, you can use your travel time as an opportunity to hone your quick-sketching skills.

Don't worry about making a recognisable composition; instead try to capture as much as you possibly can from what you see out of the window. Make a series of speedy marks and lines that represent every tree, intersection, street sign, traffic light and animal that passes. You may not have time to arrange the positioning of each addition to your drawing, so enjoy the free and abstract aesthetic of the resulting artwork. By the time you finish a journey and a drawing, there may well be some discernible observations on the paper, but overall you should have an energetic mass of lines and strokes that act as a diary entry for the trip.

Log your trips

Make a single drawing on one side of a sheet for each journey, and when you have finished, note down the origin and destination on the reverse of the drawing. The sketchbook will soon fill up and become a visual log of your journeys, and it might stop you reverting to your inner child who repeatedly asks, 'Are we there yet?'

SEEING THE BIGGER PICTURE

It's not only clouds up there. Make a drawing of everything happening above your head, noting down on paper the tops of buildings and trees, flocks of birds, and the movement of planes and vapour trails.

Spending time looking up and recording what you see might seem like a luxury – when we are outside, we tend to spend most of our time rushing around, trying to get to our destinations – but there is an abundance of visual stimulation to enjoy when looking up at the sky. And of course you can always tell yourself that drawing outside is a good way of getting some vitamin D.

Vary the pressure

If you have one, use a soft pencil to replicate the delicate edges and shadows of the clouds and the gradation of tone in the sky. Change the direction and level of pressure that you apply with the tip and the edge of the graphite, and use your finger or an eraser to blend and smooth the shadows.

Use a firmer pressure on the pencil as well as different gestures and marks to add the networks of condensation trails left by aircraft, for example, or the dark silhouettes of birds flying by.

Frame the drawing with confident lines and scratches to represent the branches of trees, lampposts and the tops of buildings. This is similar to how you might give depth to a landscape drawing by building up the background, middle ground and foreground.

You can try making the image as a circular polyorama by arranging all of the visual events you want to get down on paper around a central point, in a style akin to a photomontage or collage.

CAPTURE THE SUN

Enjoy time in the sun while making a drawing that is only revealed after some help from its rays.

First, do not look directly at the sun! It may sound obvious, but it is worth saying. Instead use the sun to make a drawing in the form of a cyanotype, or photogram. For this, you will need to buy a cyanotype kit. Make a silhouette on photographic paper by covering areas of the paper with objects, or create a drawing using a marker pen on acetate, then expose the paper to the sun. Run water over the paper and watch the image develop as it dries. You will be left with an image made with the help of the sun's ultraviolet light.

A DANCE ON PAPER

Imagine that all the people moving through a busy, lively environment are dancers in a production that you are choreographing. Let your pen follow the way each person moves as you record their actions on paper.

Everyone has their own set of movements and individual traits, which you can try to capture with a unique set of marks. Next time you are sitting down for a coffee in a café, waiting for a train, in the queue at the supermarket or having lunch in the park, take a look at all the people moving within and passing through the space around you. Someone may be making small movements with their arms as they read a magazine, another might be striding purposefully towards a destination, and another may be tapping their foot impatiently at a counter.

Use your pen to follow the way each person moves and map their trajectory within the space. You can do this exercise for a minute or you can keep working on the one sheet of paper in one location for several hours.

Different strokes

Use a different mark to represent each person. Assign individual dancers a colour or drawing implement (from pencil, to pen, to charcoal, to eyeliner, to highlighter). It might be easiest and most effective to focus solely on individuals' movements rather than on the paper and the composition of your drawing. You should end up with a set of choreographer's marks or perhaps something that resembles a musical score, based on the way a group of individuals have interacted in this one space at one time. The chances are, your dancers will not even have realised their part in the production that you have just transcribed.

CHALLENGES MAKE YOU FEEL GOOD

Remember those mazes that would come on a paper placemat when you went for pizza as a child? Try designing your own, but make it as complicated and as nearly impossible to crack as you can. Invent as many spirals, wrong turns and dead ends as you can fit on the page, and then ask the cleverest person you know to complete the challenge.

To create your own maze, you will need a sheet of paper and a black pen. Remember that the bigger the sheet of paper that you work on, the more complex the maze you can create. Start from the final destination point of the maze, which can be in the centre of the paper or anywhere on the sheet that you wish, and draw a celebratory symbol to signify the completion of a difficult journey. Work your way outwards from the end point with your pen. Create as many dead ends and wrong turns as you can fit on the page and make the players double-back on themselves, go round in circles and get lost.

The pathway you are designing doesn't necessarily have to go in straight lines with right angles and sharp corners. Use spirals, coils, twists and turns to confuse and infuriate anyone trying to crack the maze. Think of unusual methods to trick the eye and the mind into taking a wrong path, and encourage a participant to continue to travel the wrong way towards an abrupt stop.

Make copies of the maze and see which of your friends and family can complete it.

DRAW A SYMPHONY

Imagine you are a composer who wants to create a musical score of all the sounds around you at this minute. Tune in to the way various sounds make you feel and create a visual expression of each. Think about how you will represent a crash, a beep, a ticking or a gentle hum, and then put it to paper.

By using symbols, shapes and gestures, you can attempt to draw the sounds occurring around you. Just for one minute, listen carefully: even if it seems quiet, there will be numerous soft audible happenings created by machines, nature and other humans.

Then try to separate each sound into its own compartment, as if each different noise is coming from an individual instrument in an orchestra or a voice in a choir.

You may hear the background noise of a fan or a motorbike in the distance, a car honking its horn or the ticking of a clock. Without drawing the sources of these sounds – the fan, the motorbike, the car or the clock – find a way to illustrate the humming, purring, beeping and tick-tocking using a pencil and paper.

Use a kind of visual onomatopoeia to replicate these sounds by creating shapes, marks, swishes, jabs, orbs, scratches and dotted lines with your pencil on paper. Try to create the effect of a cacophony of dissonant sounds or a harmonious chorus of everyday objects. Think of how a conductor and orchestra might process the visual information you have given them and how they might recreate the one-minute's worth of noise that you have scored.

MONEY WITH MEANING

Inject some fun and creativity into an everyday object and draw your own personalised currency, complete with values, security strips and a watermark.

What if you were to make your own currency – one that didn't conform to the denominations that we would expect? Instead of five-, ten-, twenty- and fifty-pound notes, you could tailor each note to fit its intended purpose, whether it was to buy a bottle of orange juice from the shop, a half-hour French lesson, a second-hand desk from a friend or dinner for four in the best restaurant in town. Rather than standing as a promise of money, it will have a value in itself, one that is worth more than the paper it has been drawn on.

A bespoke exchange

When you are given cash, what you are being given is essentially an IOU – a promise to pay the bearer of that monetary token the value stated on the piece of paper or metal disc. That note or coin is only really worth its weight in metal or paper, and acts as an agreement to settle up later.

Humans have bartered for millennia, and still do. One person will swap an object or a service for another and, when possible, will store some IOUs for a rainy day.

Note-worthy elements

Measure a note to ascertain the dimensions for your own paper cash. Using a scalpel, ruler and cutting mat, or a pair of scissors, cut a sheet of paper into several note-sized strips. Before starting to draw on the strips of paper, keep in mind that this note should be worth the exchange for the other party. Give yourself the best chance possible that they will accept this artwork in exchange for goods or services rendered.

The design of a real note generally includes a numerical value; a portrait of a famous person; an intricately designed background made up of hatching, cross-hatching, loops and swirls; security strips; and a watermark. Use these elements and their placement to guide your own design. With a pencil, lightly map out the placement of the components on the paper, and then with a fine black pen, work on the outlines, graphic shapes, patterns and any words or numbers. Shade in any areas with a pencil to give depth and roundness to the different components in your composition. To create a watermark, use a pencil to lightly apply a shaded image. With your finger, rub a little water on the reverse side of the paper, behind the image. Your rubbing should remove part of the surface of the paper. Done well, this should give an impressive watermark effect.

Now that you have your bartering token, see if you can make an exchange. The other person can always say no, and if they do, just remind yourself, 'It's their loss!' But perhaps bring some real cash as a backup, just in case.

CREATIVE DINING

The next time you invite friends to your home to share a meal, ensure the atmosphere is fun by setting a creative table and giving your guests something unique to put their plates on.

Using a large sketchpad or loose sheets of lightweight paper and different coloured markers, make a number of quick sketches that will become placemats for a future dinner party or family meal. If you know all of the guests who will be sitting at your table, draw a speedy portrait of each of them, decorating the edges of the sheets with references to their interests and characteristics. The diners' placemats can also serve as place-setting cards, and they will each have to decide which seat is theirs based on your representation of them.

Coasters and cloth

Next, take a large single sheet of paper and cut out one small square per placemat. Illustrate a particular feature of each of your guests on the squares to make coasters.

To create a tablecloth, fill a long length of paper with loose designs for the table – marking out locations for the cutlery, serving bowls, candlesticks and water jug. Go maximalist and embellish the designs with geometric shapes or confident gestures. The size of paper needed will depend on the length of your table and the number of visitors you are expecting; it may be easiest to purchase a roll of paper from an art-materials shop.

It might be the first time your guests will have eaten on a multi-layered, table-based artwork. When the meal is finished, they can even take home their individualised placemats – as long as they are not messy eaters.

A MARK-MAKING JOURNEY

Turn a long walk into an artistic journey.

Every one hundred steps you take, document something that stands out so that it becomes part of the story of your journey. Rather than listing these small events and observations using words, do so using small drawings that visually describe what you have seen and experienced. You will end up with an alternative map of your expedition. Even if you were to repeat this exercise over and over again on exactly the same journey, the map you would create would be different each time.

MAKE A CADAVRE EXQUIS WITH FRIENDS

Try this fun game to encourage creativity and motivate you and your friends to collaborate on fashioning the most grotesque creature imaginable.

The phrase *cadavre exquis* translates as 'exquisite corpse'. This may sound gruesome (and the results often can be), but it is actually a fun drawing game that was invented by artists in the early twentieth century. It can be played by two or more people.

The first person draws the head of a person, creature or beast at the top of a piece of paper, and then carefully folds the paper over the drawing, concealing it from the next player, but leaving visible the lines where the neck might connect to the rest of the body.

The next player then continues the drawing by concentrating on the chest area, folds it over, and then passes the drawing on again, leaving the guide lines for the next player. The game continues with the drawing moving on to the stomach, then the thighs, calves and feet. The players may draw a chicken's wattle, a skeleton's rib cage, an ogre's hairy knees and an elephant's feet.

By the end of the game, the paper is full (perhaps with six or so sequential drawings), and no player will have seen any more than the elements they have drawn themselves.

At this point, the sheet of paper can be unfolded and the hideous creation revealed. The idea is to make each part of the exquisite corpse as gruesome, surreal and funny as possible!

A LIFE OF ADVENTURE

Some artists feel at their most confident working in the comfort (or often discomfort) of a studio. Other artists prefer to work *en plein air*, carrying their materials with them. Be adventurous and find unusual places in which to draw from life.

Make the most of sketching's portability by choosing locations you never thought of sketching in before, and carry a book with you to capture unexpected moments. One of the best things about sketching is how easy it is to do in places that would be near impossible if painting in oil or acrylic. There is no need to carry easels, paints, drying oils, brushes, rags and solvents. There is also no mess from splashed and dripped colour, no turpentine to harm your lungs and no need to wait for days – or even months – for your artwork to dry. All you need is an implement to mark with and a surface to mark on.

This opens up many possibilities when it comes to where you can make an artwork. The fact that pencils and paper are so portable means that

you can stealthily invade locations that would be much more difficult with a cumbersome kit full of painting materials and tools.

Dare to sketch

Be creative about where you draw. Start a series of artworks made in unusual places and try drawing from life when travelling in a car, walking on a tightrope, making a skydive, working through a tour of duty on a submarine or when swimming (make sure you get some waterproof paper for the last one).

They say a change is as good as a rest, so this exercise can give you a boost and get you out of a rut any time you feel stuck.

THE BEAUTY OF A SINGLE MOMENT

Embrace the energy and action of a busy scene.

Whether you are in a crowd or in a busy restaurant, concentrate and observe all that is happening in a particular moment in that particular place. In just one second, take in every movement, every interaction, every smile and every sound. Then take your time to capture all of these happenings on paper. Without realising it, you will be filling in the gaps and creating a new story from this single moment.

CELEBRATE YOUR DAY

When you get a minute in the evening, before you go to bed, trace your way back through all the events of the day in the form of a linear drawing, illustrating key moments that you want to remember.

Treat this exercise as if you are making a timeline of the history of your day as a way of processing everything you have accomplished in the past sixteen or so hours. Without lifting your pen from the paper, start with the moment you wake up and, working from left to right, draw small, simple symbols and scenarios in one continuous line.

The accomplishments of your day may be impressive, such as passing your driving test or getting a promotion, or they may be made up of a number of micro-victories, such as making a perfect pancake or remembering to pick up a new tube of toothpaste from the supermarket.

In chronological order, link every mini milestone, from making breakfast, to getting on the bus, through to doing the washing up after dinner, and finish with yourself making this drawing.

Give your linear drawing a cohesive aesthetic. If you work neatly using small details, you might be able to fit a whole week's worth of daily timelines down the length of the page. At the end of the week you will be able to look back and see what is consistent in your life and how tight or loose your daily routine is. Annotate these timelines with words and thoughts to describe what was positive about certain moments and achievements.

PERSONAL MAIL

The next time you send a postcard or letter to someone you know, draw your own stamp next to the postage stamp on the envelope, and try to make it look as realistic as possible. This exercise is a wonderful way to share hidden and significant messages, and to send good vibes to other people.

Before drawing your own stamp, you need to mark out where it will go on the envelope. Use the official stamp to do this, placing it slightly to the left of where it will eventually sit. With a sharp pencil, very lightly trace around the shape of the stamp. You can then attach the stamp in its final, usual position.

Using a sharp coloured pencil, draw a portrait within the drawn outline, attempting to match the scale of the profile (if there is one) on the original stamp. Make a portrait of yourself, or a friend, as royalty. Use gentle shading to give roundness to the cheeks and shape to the hair. Imagine you have sculpted the face from clay and then rendered it in two dimensions. If you are feeling especially regal, add a crown and embellish it to the point that it would make real royalty jealous.

If you would prefer not to draw a portrait, use the design of the original stamp for inspiration and hide a coded message for the recipient within the drawing. Use symbols and words that will only be significant to the receiver. Your envelope is now a work of art that can be kept and treasured by the recipient.

IMAGINE YOUR PERFECT PLACE

One of the great things about drawing is that you can create places, people and situations that don't exist. Or, at least, don't exist yet! Use drawing as a tool to visualise your dreams and become the architect of a place that you have always wished you could visit. Whether it is a house, a city or an undiscovered planet, design it down to the last detail, even if you work on it little by little over days, weeks or months.

This exercise in drawing detail begins by visualising a place that is the very embodiment of perfection. You could imagine the most beautiful building that you could ever live in, or your spot could be an amalgamation of the most stunning landscapes and seascapes that you have encountered during your life. Or it could be a more abstract experience that will take some careful thought when it comes to visual depiction.

Start to map out this place in the form of a drawing, and rather than sketching out the whole scene in one sitting, think of the artwork as an ongoing project. The idea of your perfect place can be fluid; changes and evolution can be represented by adding to your drawing or manipulating it. Details can also be added to transform the mood and atmosphere of the picture.

When it comes to drawing there is usually something to be said for working quickly, thinking fast and acting on your first impressions. Many of the exercises in this book encourage immediate responses and instant results. However, with this exercise there is no rush – it can be worked and reworked indefinitely.

DRAW YOUR FUTURE

Visualise yourself, or someone close to you, in the future. Make a portrait of that future self. Don't just think of how hair, skin and teeth may change over time; consider all the ways in which appearance may have altered, including clothes, posture, personal technology and style.

This portrait from the future should start with a close look at yourself in the mirror (or at a friend, if you prefer). Imagine you have travelled forward twenty, forty or fifty years. Start to sketch, thinking about what will be different and how you might look. Will your hair have changed from black to grey? Will the laughter lines around your eyes have become more pronounced? Will you have more hairs in your ears or fewer hairs on your head? Do you think you might be wiser, stronger and more confident later in life?

Take into account all of these changes in your appearance and use the face in front of you as a guide. When it comes to your clothes, try to imagine the fashions you might be following: perhaps a spacesuit, a robotic prosthetic, a zoot suit or post-apocalyptic tattered-rags chic.

Complete your portrait by adding futuristic technology and a background that hints at what the planet might look like by that time. Will you be living in the same place with the same wallpaper, or will you be living in a domestic pod at the bottom of the ocean? Will humans have populated Mars?

CELEBRATE YOUR ACHIEVEMENTS

Fill a diary with a year of daily visual entries. Every time something exciting or unusual happens, make a drawing.

Keep a diary of small drawings depicting all the exciting moments of each day. When you have completed a whole year's worth of entries, make a habit of referring to the drawings from the same date of the previous year to remind you of everything you have achieved and observed.

VISUALISE YOUR PERFECT SPACE

Redesign the room you are in as you think it should be, perhaps adding a cinema screen, a chandelier and a shark tank.

By sketching out the room that you are in now, you can then think about how you could make it more imaginative – with unusual additions, alternative uses of the space or different furniture. Whether you are in a house, a hotel, a restaurant or a library, the design and furnishings may well be mostly functional. Sofas face TVs, chairs sit next to tables, lights hang from ceilings, and pictures hang on walls. Of course there is a reason for this, and most of these rooms might serve their purpose relatively well. Does the room you are in right now inspire you? Does it excite you or stimulate conversation or encourage creative thinking?

In your preliminary sketch, mark out lines that give the room perspective from your current viewing position. Alternatively, you can make a floor plan, as if you were looking down from above.

Now be creative and come up with a less utilitarian, more inspiring use of the space.

No limits

Draw all the unusual, extravagant, fantastical objects, creatures and features that could populate every wall, floor, ceiling, nook and cranny. Think about how each addition could relate to the others, and whether it could fit some purpose or perform some function. Features needn't simply be things to sit on, eat from or keep you warm. Think instead about what could encourage you to interact with someone, inspire you to learn how to dance, help you to let off some steam or live out a lifelong dream of being a comic villain.

Design inward-facing circular seating, add monkey bars to swing from or an ice luge for penguins sweeping through the room. There's nothing holding you back creatively.

SKETCH YOUR BEST SELF

Everyone seems to be embarrassed by their passport photo, so draw a self-portrait at passport-photo size that represents you as you would like to be seen.

Cut a piece of paper to the same size as an official passport photo. Set up a mirror in front of you and then, using a pencil, get to work on a realistic, but not-too-realistic, self-portrait. Accentuate or soften any features you want to change and create a version of yourself as you would like to be seen. Give yourself bigger muscles, longer hair, more freckles and a dimple in your chin, and accessorise with fake eyelashes, big hoop earrings or a facial tattoo.

When you have finished your drawing, using clear, self-adhesive sheets, laminate the miniature self-portrait to make it seem as authentic as possible. Keep your alternative passport photo in your wallet or purse and bring it out when your friends are laughing at each other's official passport photos. It's probably best to keep your personalised portrait for less official eyes, as it might not go down so well when travelling or renewing your driver's licence.

GIFT YOUR LOVE OF DRAWING

Next time you give someone a book, personalise it with your own illustration as a surprise for the recipient.

An empty book page can be an ideal space to draw your own illustration based on the contents and ideas within the story. Most novels have at least one blank page at the front or back of the book. These empty pages can be very useful for the reader as a space in which to write notes or perhaps a message if the book is being given as a gift – or, even better, as a space for your very own interpretative artwork.

Know your medium

Before you start working on your illustrated artwork, check the paper stock that has been used. Test out a small section of a page in an inconspicuous area by applying a little ink from a pen, and a few marks from pencils with a range of different degrees of softness. This will let you know how absorbent the surface is, how well the materials work together, and whether your pen's ink will blot, spread or seep through the next five sheets.

A personal reading

Once you have decided which drawing implement is best suited to the surface, start working on an illustration. You may decide to draw an alternate cover image for the book, or your interpretation of the book's themes and characters. The resulting image can be as simple or as complex as you want and should reflect your response to the contents.

When your friend has finished reading the book, ask whether your illustration influenced, contextualised or affected the way that they responded to the story.

SHARE YOUR CREATIVITY

Rather than accumulating piles of sketches, when you finish a drawing put a stamp on it and address it to someone you know.

A great way to gain an audience for your creative work is by sending your artworks to your friends. If you were to work through every exercise in this book you would be left with hundreds of drawings. Some may take a few seconds to complete; others you may end up working on for days, weeks or even months. It is most likely that you will have sketches in books, on loose sheets of paper, on the backs of postcards and on many other surfaces. These drawings may be lying around your home, neatly tucked away in a portfolio or kept in boxes.

As well as the joy found in the act of drawing itself, there is also the joy of letting other people see something that you have created. You can fold the sheets of paper and put them in envelopes; carefully package them in acid-free tissue or archival sleeves and send them in card-backed packaging; or simply stick a stamp directly on a drawing, write the address on the front or back of the paper, and let the postal mark and any marks gained during its journey become interesting additions to the artwork.

If you have created a portrait of a friend, think about giving it to them, as long as it isn't too unflattering. Rather than sending a birthday card, think about sending a drawing instead. Let go of some of these creative moments and give them a new life somewhere else.

BUILD A WORLD

If you have ever been to the theatre you may have noticed how much thought and skill has gone into the design and fabrication of the stage set, and how effective it is in setting the scene. Take control and begin the adventure of building your own tiny world.

Design your own stage set – either based on a story you know well or one that you create from your imagination. The stage can be based on a famous theatre on Broadway in New York or in the West End in London, or on a space or room you know very well, such as your bedroom or living room.

A cast of thousands

Most major theatres and opera houses have a team of skilled people working on creating the sets. There will most likely be a scenic artists' department, a carpentry department and a metalwork department, as well as a team of lighting technicians and sound engineers, all working alongside each other to make a new performance space for the actors, dancers and singers for each new production.

Skills, materials and time are utilised to realise a vast, stage-sized version of a comparatively small plan or *maquette* created by an artist or set designer. The original design may only be as big as a large dictionary, but will contain all of the important features to be replicated on a grand scale by the team of craftspeople, technicians and creatives.

Building the scene

To work on your own set design, begin by mapping out the empty stage. You can choose the scale and base this design on an impressive theatre you have visited before or on a small room that you are familiar with. Within the space, and working with perspective, create the *mise en scène* by starting to populate the different areas with backdrops, props, lighting sources, furniture and all the intricate details that will help you to convey the desired atmosphere.

If you are feeling bold, make a *maquette* of your set. Begin by constructing the three walls and the floor of the stage, and then draw and cut out each element (the curtains, the flooring, a door and a window). Make the scene three-dimensional by paying attention to the foreground, middle ground and background, trying to convey a sense of distance and perspective by making the cutout elements progressively smaller as they move towards the background. Try drawing on different materials, including canvas for the backdrop, fabric for the curtains, laminate for the flooring and black card to represent a night sky. You may choose to make the set from a lightweight foam-core board with balsa wood that has been cut and glued to create staircases, frames and ladders. Use pencils, pens and markers to shade, cross-hatch and darken areas to add drama to background landscapes, character to actor silhouettes, and details and texture to trees and plants. Try to give the whole scene as much character and personality as the actors who will perform within it.

A CREATIVE CLOSE TO THE DAY

Just before going to bed, make a quick sketch of something you want to remember from today or something you wish to achieve tomorrow.

As the late evening can be a very creative time of day for many people, use it to sketch out important moments from the previous twenty-four hours. This does not need to be in the form of a list – it can be a loose, gestural way of working out what needs to be remembered and pondered.

If you are one of those people whose mind is still busy running through the events of the day when lying in bed, this activity is a good way of getting those thoughts down on paper, which can help you wind down before going to sleep.

Alternatively, use this sketching technique to begin to think of what you want to achieve tomorrow.

A free hand

Let your hand make marks on the paper even before you have a clear idea of where the drawing is heading. Letting go of a direct, conscious train of thought can lead to an unexpected epiphany. You may also continue to process the ideas captured in your drawing while you sleep, and, if you are lucky, you'll wake up in the morning with a creative solution to any problem or task.

There is more than one exercise in this book that can be undertaken while in bed, so it might make sense to have a dedicated paper pad that is kept on your bedside table or under your pillow.

ENJOY THE MINUSCULE

Stretch your creative repertoire and expand your artistic skills by using the end of a pin rather than paint and a brush to make your own pointillist artwork. This is the perfect way to unwind.

Use the point of a pin as a drawing tool and prick numerous tiny holes in a sheet of paper to create an intricate masterpiece. Alter the size of the holes by changing the pressure you apply. You can then lay a second sheet under your detailed artwork and rub a stick of charcoal over the holes to produce a soft impression of your perforated original.

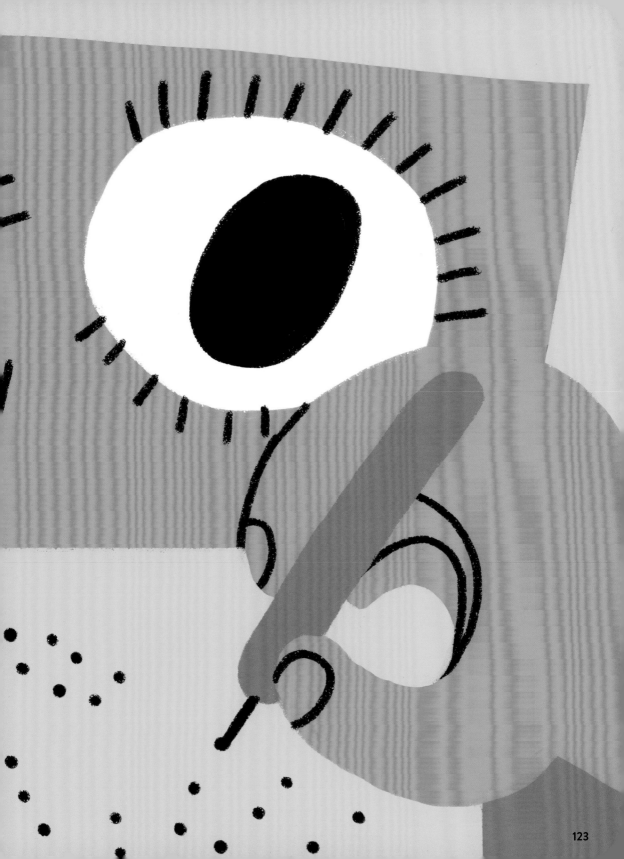

MAKE A SCULPTURAL DRAWING

Many sculptors use drawing as a tool to develop ideas for three-dimensional artworks. If you haven't done this before, learning a new skill can be very freeing.

Add this skill to your artistic toolbox by planning and designing your own sculpture using pencils, pens or charcoal, and paper. Shading, cross-hatching and varied pressure can be used to reflect the curves, contours and angles of a potential sculptural object. Before starting your sculpture plan, choose your surface. How do you want your drawing to be seen? Does the aesthetic work better on card, wood, plasterboard, plastic or the back of an envelope rather than a sheet of white paper? Does the surface correspond to the materials you might use to construct your sculpture?

Free rein

When choosing what you want to portray, remember that your drawing does not necessarily have to represent the smooth anatomical contours of a marble bust, or an abstracted figure made in bronze. Instead, it can be a study of natural or man-made forms, a hybrid built of different objects, or something non-physical. The underside of a car, the contents of a toolbox, a roll of masking tape or a pile of rubbish can be just as fascinating to explore as more traditional subjects.

Build depth

Give your drawing a full sculptural effect by using your drawing tool to gouge, scrape, brush, etch and mark your chosen surface to represent texture, shape, form and colour. Try to represent the subject as three-dimensional; consider the way light will reflect and shadows will fall, and use these elements to bring the object to life. Don't be afraid to use colour and additional collage materials to help this two-dimensional artwork to embody all the characteristics that you want to portray in the planned three-dimensional form.

SKETCH YOUR COMMUTE

Bring creativity to your commute by allowing the movement of your journey to direct your pencil and create a series of travel drawings.

The next time you are making a journey, whether you are commuting to work or taking a train to visit a friend, open your sketchpad or notebook on your lap and gently rest the tip of your pen or pencil on the surface. Let the turns, starts, stops and bumps form their own drawings and become a record of the journey. The bumpier the ride, the better.

DEEP IN THE DETAILS

Improve your perception and realign your focus by developing an awareness of small details in the built environment. By capturing the way bricks interlock, the texture of cement, the arc of a span of steel and the grain in wood frames, it is possible to draw a building brick by brick rather than sketching a series of large characterless shapes.

In this exercise, draw your chosen segment of building as if you were a bricklayer, building each wall one brick, one layer, at a time. While you can create a very effective impression of a building by using shading, hatching and confident angular marks to describe the geometry and shapes of its architecture, another approach is to look closely at the materials that make the building and give it its character.

Use a series of carefully considered pencil marks to depict each interlocking block and the sliver of cement where each brick joins the next. If you want to keep your lines and angles moving along in the right direction, you can lightly mark out the geometric shapes of the corners of the walls using a ruler and pencil. Alternatively, you can embrace working more freely and just draw from brick to brick, enjoying the looser results. When you approach doors, window frames and drainage pipes, change your mark-making style. Replicate the smoothness of glass or the roundness of a pipe through shading, smudging and gently erasing marks – this will allow you to mirror the texture and finish of each material.

When it comes to the bricks, try not to simply draw a series of rectangles. When you look closely at each brick you will notice how the colour and texture changes along its length. To make the building come alive, use the tip and the edge of your pencil to represent the changing tones, marks and finish of each brick.

NEW PERSPECTIVE

The next time you draw a room, the view from your window, or a landscape, try reversing perspective by bringing the buildings or objects in the distance to the foreground, visually describing them in detail and pushing everything in the foreground into the distance. This exercise is a great way to practise seeing in a new way.

Trying to create a drawing that plays with the existing perspective and positioning of everything in your view is quite a complicated exercise, and you may need a few attempts to get it right. If you were to look out of a window onto a cityscape, the view might contain a long road flanked by trees and skyscrapers, reaching out towards the horizon. As you look out to the distance you will see the diminishing perspective, with the buildings seemingly reducing in size the further they get from your eyes.

Bring the buildings that are furthest away in the distance to the fore of your drawing, and push the closest buildings, trees and even the curtains in your room back towards the skyline. Switch the perspective of the road by drawing it as widening rather than narrowing as it stretches out into the distance.

This exercise does not have to have a cityscape as its subject. Try it with your own views, which may be of a rural landscape, a row of shops or even the interior of the room you are in. Vary your approach to disrupting the perspective of certain scenes and discover complex ways of confusing the viewers with your drawings.

A MAP TO TAKE YOU HOME

You may have made the same journey home hundreds or even thousands of times. Perhaps you are usually focused on the road, a book or your own thoughts, but somehow you can make it home without even thinking about it. Consciously shift your focus and try to draw a map of your journey, remembering every turn, traffic light, obstacle and memorable building.

For this task, you need to act as a cartographer, mapping out a whole journey on a single sheet of paper. You also need to be a tourist on your commute home, whether it's from college, work or the local shops. Look around you and pay attention to all the things you would normally overlook while you are thinking, listening, riding or driving. Note every turn, every fork in the road and every traffic light. Keep a mental note of the location of any memorials, public sculptures, giant trees or fire stations. Is there always someone playing music in the same spot every day or the same man with a big grey beard having a coffee on a table outside the local café?

Chart new territory

Be creative in how you represent the changes in direction, the landmarks and the unique buildings and people that will make the map easier to follow.

Don't worry about working to scale; shorten or lengthen stretches of road to allow for the inclusion of visual descriptions or more detail on your map. Don't forget to record small variations in the colour or texture of the surroundings, like the difference in brickwork on the buildings from one street to the next.

More than the sights

You don't have to restrict yourself to recording what you see. Perhaps there is a particular smell at one

point of your journey – fresh bread outside the bakery, or the mixture of engine oil and solvent you inhale when passing the mechanics' workshop. Or maybe there is the sound of Turkish music always playing from a local restaurant, or bells chiming on the hour coming from a church. Illustrate these scents and sounds within the drawing, too, remembering they should not be one-off occurrences but reliable sensory clues to help someone follow the map.

Test your skills
Give the map to someone who does not know the route you take to get home and challenge them to follow your artistic directions. You could always incentivise them with the offer of a reward in the form of dinner or a drink when they arrive – a small prize for successfully finding their way to you.

EXPLORE WHAT IS INSIDE

Take a look at an object, a building or a person. Rather than drawing what you can see on the surface, use your imagination to picture what is within. Perhaps the interior has a real effect on the texture or shape of the exterior.

Channel your inner Leonard da Vinci and practise the exercise of learning what lies beneath the visible surface of your subjects, to further inform your drawings. If you look closely at Leonardo's paintings, drawings and anatomical studies, you will see how his approach to portraying the human form was both scientific and artistic. He clearly understood what was going on underneath the skin of his subjects and utilised this knowledge to great effect. Similarly, George Stubbs's paintings of horses in the eighteenth century are highly realistic because of their sophisticated visual descriptions of the muscles, tendons and ligaments lying beneath the animals' skins.

Approach your drawing in a similar way. Study what is within or underneath the surface of your subject and let this guide how you convey what can be seen on its surface. If you are looking at a carrier bag, inspect its contents so that you can understand why there are areas on its exterior that are more bulbous or protruding than others. If you are planning on drawing a satsuma, study the endocarp and the mesocarp before drawing the surface of the skin. If you are making a sketch of the outside of a building, have a walk around the inside and think about what effect the interior layout has had on the building's facade.

DREAMY DRAWING

It is often in the moments before going to sleep that people have some of their most lucid and inventive thoughts. Some lucky people can fall asleep the moment their head hits the pillow – this exercise is probably not for them.

Keep a pencil and a notepad or sketchbook next to your bed, by your alarm clock or under your pillow, so that they are to hand. Right before you go to sleep – during that in-between time when you are not fully awake but still able to function – make a drawing of your last conscious thought. It might be an idea that's just come to you, something on your mind from the day just gone or some kind of surrealist pre-dream. Sketch it out in a way that might be memorable or recognisable for your future self to decipher.

A treasure of ideas

Every now and then have a look back through these drawings – there might be a golden idea hidden somewhere in that sketchbook.

If you happen to be a morning person, try this exercise in reverse and make a habit of reaching for the sketchbook or notebook as you are waking up. Make a record of thoughts you have during the moments when you are becoming sentient enough to put pencil to paper.

EVERY OPPORTUNITY

Use your travel time as the perfect opportunity to put your ideas to paper.

For some people, the only time available to stop, think, listen to music or read a book is when they are in transit – on the bus, on the train, when flying or on the subway. This can also be the perfect time to draw. Make sure you take your sketchbook with you when travelling or commuting, and use that time to record any ideas, thoughts and observations on paper.

DRAWING CLARITY

Use your finger, the back of a spoon, or a brush to make a drawing using just water. The drawing will change, move and disappear as it evaporates.

Try making satisfying yet ephemeral artworks by creating drawings with water on different surfaces. For many artists, the media they work in (for example, watercolour, acrylic, oil or ink), the surfaces they work on (whether paper, canvas, wood or plastic), and the colours they use (which can be made up from organic, inorganic, lightfast or fugitive pigments or colours) all have to be archival and permanent. This means that the artworks the artists create will undergo minimal changes over the years, won't degrade and should last for lifetimes. However, it can sometimes be very liberating to make an artwork that only lasts for hours or minutes and then all but ceases to exist.

Moving images

When applying the water, the way it will behave will depend not only on the tilt and angle of the drawing surface, but also on the surface itself. Paper will absorb or repel the water, depending on the materials making up the pulp, the method of making the paper and the sizing. A heavy professional watercolour paper will allow some of the liquid to sit on its surface and will not cockle as the water is slowly absorbed. A thin copy paper will ripple and buckle in moments.

Fleeting beauty

Observe the way your image moves, spreads and disappears when applied to paper, the surface of a table, the back of a book or the palm of your hand. Try applying different liquids (such as your tea or coffee) and using different implements (say, the back of a spoon or your finger). Let the liquids evaporate and see what ghost images are left behind.

A VISUAL PLAN

Make a confident start to your day! First thing in the morning, just after waking up, make a drawing that plans out the day. The drawing can be a series of diagrams that map out your schedule, or a sketch that helps you to organise your day as a whole.

Keep a notepad or sketchbook next to your bed. Just after you have woken up and a few minutes before you need to spring out of bed and into action, plan through all the things that you need to get done over the course of the day in the form of a timeline sketch.

Many people wake up with a sense of dread, and there are probably many different factors that contribute to this. There's too much to do: work to get to, bills to pay, food to buy, people to meet.

This morning drawing exercise can be a good way of preparing yourself to venture out from under the covers and face the world outside.

A timeline can help you to visualise the order of events and prioritise each one. Start with showering or making breakfast and finish with getting back into bed.

Weighing it up
You can weight the importance of each of your things to do by making the drawings in your day plan bigger or smaller, darker or lighter, or outlined in bold, faint or dotted lines.

A written list can be hard to keep focused on – blurring into a mishmash of confusing, muddled letters on a page. Your visual plan for the day will clarify the importance of each upcoming task and help you to organise your thoughts before getting on with everything you need to do.

This exercise is a positive and creative way to start your daily routine, not to mention a great way to develop your quick-sketching skills.

REALISE BIG ASPIRATIONS

This is an opportunity to think about who you aspire to be and your hopes for the future. The drawing you make for this exercise can be representational or abstract, can depict a place where you would like to live or work, or it can be a self-portrait from a successful future. Leave the drawing in the care of someone you trust, with the instruction for it not to be opened for ten years.

Take a piece of paper and a pen, travel through time and draw an achievement from the future – as a lifelike rendering or an abstract representation. Try to create an image that words alone couldn't convey. You can draw a single object or a series of symbols that describe a way of life, or you can sketch what you think your viewpoint will be in ten years from this exact moment.

Hopes and dreams

Bill Gates said, 'Most people overestimate what they can do in one year, and underestimate what they can do in ten years.' Perhaps you have a clear idea in your head of where you want to be or what you want to have achieved in ten years. Maybe your aspirations and vision of your future aren't simple concepts.

In ten years from now, you might have amassed huge wealth or built an empire, you could have graduated from college or bought a house, you might have made one thousand new friends or made one person's life better. It could be that you have looked after your family or have spent the time being content with your life.

Think about something you hope to have achieved in ten years' time. It can be something simple or it can be something complex. It can be a feeling of happiness or inner peace, or it can be something concrete – literally or metaphorically.

This moment

When you've finished the drawing, put it to one side and try to clear your head. Now think about where you are today and how you think of yourself.

Take a new sheet of paper and start again, finding a way of using marks to portray a sense of who you are at this moment in time. Again, this can be something easily recognisable or it can be a series of symbols or objects that represent this exact moment in your life.

Take both of these sheets of paper and look at them side by side. How similar or different are they? How different is the 'you' you see in ten years' time to the 'you' you see in the present? Have you approached the way you have made marks to create each portrait in the same way?

Look to the future

Now put both drawings into an envelope and seal it. You can choose a padded, card-backed envelope or an archival box that will keep the drawings in pristine condition; or you can fold them up and seal them in whatever envelope you have lying around (anything you can safely seal and post is fine, even if it is second hand; just make sure to tape it closed).

On the back of the envelope write: 'Do not open until ten years from receipt, and only open with the sender present.'

Send the envelope to someone who can be trusted not to accidentally lose, throw away or burn it. Ten years from now, you may have to reconnect with the guardian of the drawings. Together, you will be able to see if you have become and achieved what you wanted to, if your aspirations have changed, and how much of a difference ten years have made.

KEEP ON MOVING

Change the way you make your marks on paper. Let your non-dominant hand do the work and make a picture by dragging the sheet and not the pencil. It's good to give your weaker hand a workout once in a while and prove to yourself you can do things you didn't think possible.

Start by setting down a large sheet of paper or sketchpad. This will give you more room to manoeuvre when you let your non-dominant hand take charge and will stop you from running one hand into the other. Then, rather than using your more dexterous hand to hold the pen or pencil and make marks on the sheet of paper, use that hand solely to hold your drawing implement in a fixed position, touching the paper lightly to start with. Now use the fingers on your other hand to gently grasp the edge of the paper, or flatten your palm and press down on the face of the sheet, and move the page, allowing the stationary tip to make the drawing.

Look at what is in front of you and, using your non-dominant hand, drag the paper to follow and record the shapes of the forms and silhouettes you can see.

Art in motion

Propel the paper forward, sweep it backward, or drag it smoothly from under the tip of the stationary pencil. Replicate the sensation of the textures and outlines of the objects you are drawing by mirroring this in the manner in which you manipulate the drawing surface.

Your natural drawing hand doesn't have to be completely motionless. It can play a creative part in the drawing process by applying more or less downward pressure, or by tilting the angle of the pencil, to alter the depth and tone of the marks being made.

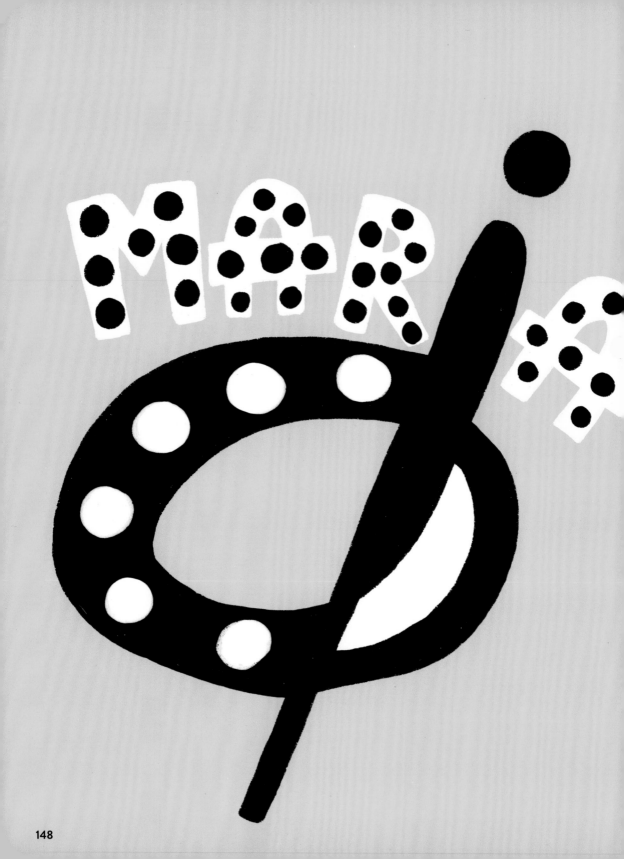

YOUR UNIQUE MARK

Just as every person's signature is different – with different dots, loops, lines, flicks and applications of pressure – so too is everyone's drawing style. Embrace the elements that reflect your character and style to craft an artistic monogram.

For your very own monogram, start signing your name and continue the gesture into a new picture. If the motion you use to create your signature is full of gentle curves and spirals then let that be reflected in your drawing. If you write your name with swift, pointed movements, then mirror that in your approach to this exercise.

MIRROR IMAGE

Use this exercise as a way of boosting your confidence in drawing with your non-dominant hand.

Choose a subject, whether it is your cooked breakfast, the contents of your wardrobe or your own face. Now gently fold a sheet of paper vertically, to create a faint line that divides the sheet lengthwise into two halves. Draw your chosen subject on one side of the paper with your dominant hand. Now, using your non-dominant hand – the hand that usually does little more than hold the paper still – make a mirror image on the other half of the paper. Try this again tomorrow and see if, over time, you can make yourself more ambidextrous.

CREATE SOLUTIONS

Drawing is another way to describe mark making. Leave your sketchbook and pencils at home and find other surfaces and materials with which to make your mark.

It's time to take an experimental approach and keep your eyes peeled for exciting and unusual objects that can become an intrinsic part of your artworks. Why not draw in the sand, on a tree, on a bus ticket or on your clothes? In the spirit of experimentation, don't restrict yourself to using a pen or pencil. Draw with your food; with rocks and mud; with your hair, fingers or elbows; or by using a fish bone and dipping ink.

For thousands of years, humans have left their marks on the walls of caves, on the sides of hills and engraved into the surface of rocks. It is only relatively recently that we have made a habit of using thin sheets of flexible materials as the go-to surface for most of our mark making. Whether it is vellum, parchment, cheap copy paper, cotton-based watercolour paper, wood pulp or mixed cellulose materials, we feel comfortable sketching, writing, drawing and doodling on these surfaces. After all, they are lightweight, flat and mostly inexpensive. In addition, archival paper, stored under the correct conditions, can last for many hundreds of years.

There are, however, countless surfaces in the world that are wonderful to draw on.

Working together

Bear in mind that your drawing media should be compatible with the surfaces you want to draw on. Take into account how porous the material you want to draw on is, so that the inks or pencil lines don't give unwanted, unexpected results. Also, remember that the colour of an object may have an effect on the colour of the ink, pencil or crayon you are using, especially if the marks being made are partially transparent. If a surface is very rough, it can damage soft- or brush-nibbed pens, and if the surface is very smooth, certain materials will slip and slide when being applied and won't adhere properly. The medium used to hold colour pigment acts as a kind of glue, keeping the colour distribution even and helping it to 'stick' to the surface you are applying it to.

Make it stick

You can always use an artist's acrylic primer on a material to give added 'tooth' and to allow ink or pencil lines to sit beautifully on the surface. A primer can also give your drawing surface a vibrant white – or any coloured – base tone. It can be bought from an art shop and applied with a brush to wood, pebbles, concrete, bricks, canvas, plastic, plaster and numerous other materials that you can find in everyday life.

The best thing to do is to experiment and to enjoy the unusual results that may occur.

A SHOPPING ADVENTURE

Instead of using words, make quick drawings of each of the items on your shopping list. It is fun to send someone to the shop with a list of this kind and see whether they are able to get every item without ending up purchasing cat food instead of tuna or an orange rather than a tomato.

Fill a sheet of scrap paper with miniature drawings of everything you need to pick up at the shop. Picture all of the ingredients, toiletries and pantry staples you need for the coming week. What do you visualise when you think of those products?

Play with the structure of the shopping list by grouping each category of food in a hierarchy, perhaps putting the things you can't do without at the top of a pyramid, followed by fruit and vegetables, carbohydrates, and then food for the dog. Or group ingredients according to each dish you will be making in the coming week, with herbs, oil and salt (which you will be using multiple times) as the crossover in a Venn diagram of foodstuffs.

Test shopper

If you are not going to be doing the shopping yourself, give the piece of paper, full of food symbols and hieroglyphics, to the shopper, whether that person is a partner, family member or roommate, and see how well they do. If your shopper is able to follow your instructions you will know your drawings have worked!

CREATIVE DIRECTIONS

Try this creative way of addressing an envelope: draw a map leading to your letter's final destination and see if it actually makes it to the recipient.

When you next send a letter or a birthday card to a friend living in a location that you know well, don't write the full address on the envelope. Instead, write only the name of the town and the postcode and then draw a map for the postal worker to follow. Start from a local landmark and visually describe the directions to the letterbox in the form of a drawing. It's probably not such a good idea to do this when sending an important document or a cash gift in a birthday card!

This is a fun way to build confidence in your abilities as an artist – and to brighten a postal worker's day.

EXPRESS YOUR FINEST MOMENT

Make a drawing that recreates an event you are particularly proud of, whether you achieved something extraordinary, made a positive difference to someone's life or created something beautiful.

Using a pencil and paper, create a sketched tableau based on your recollections of an important event. Your drawing may look like a scene from a play or a storyboard for a film you plan on making.

If you were to look back through your life, what do you think would be your finest moment? Is there a major personal achievement that played a pivotal role in your development? Maybe you created a beautiful home or a new human being, or you ran faster or jumped higher than you ever had before. Perhaps you showed kindness to someone who was in need of help or you supported a friend when they were struggling with the rent.

Revisit the memory

Picture that moment and visualise everything that was surrounding you. Try to remember who was with you, what you were wearing, whether you were inside in the warm or outside in the rain, the year the event occurred and how you felt. Capture any of the characters' facial expressions, convey the atmosphere in the location you were in, and add all the objects and props that occupied the space around you. Be as detailed as you possibly can in your recreation of the scene.

Transport yourself back to that moment and cherish every element of the experience.